I Come from Immigrants

I Come from Immigrants

Poems by

Margaret Duda

For Joan,
With gratitude
for your friendship
and admiration
for your poems.
Thank you for
the great blurb!

Margaret Duda

Cover design by Paul Duda and Shay Culligan

ISBN: 978-1-63980-334-7
Library of Congress Control Number: 2023936782

Kelsay Books
502 South 1040 East, A-119
American Fork, Utah 84003
Kelsaybooks.com

For my parents,

who immigrated to America,
and gave me the opportunities
they never had in Hungary,

and for Larry, the love of my life,
who gave me four amazing children,
which led to seven incredible grandchildren,

as he encouraged my writing and loved
reading poetry with me on the banks
of lakes and streams all over the world.

Acknowledgments

Thanks to these journals and anthologies for publishing my poems:

A Love Letter (or Poem) to . . . (A Sweetycat Press): "Gondola Ride"

Around the World: Landscapes and Cityscapes (A Sweetycat Press): "Hand in the River"

Culture and Identity: THE POET (England): "The Fragility of Film," "A Mother's Courage"

Friends and Friendship: THE POET (England): "The Lone Ranger"

Lothlorien Poetry Journal: "Amber Alert in Oswego County," "Coming to America," "Flocks of Birds and Fairy Tales," "Fostering to Freedom 1906," "Gifts from a Stranger," "Hungarian Angels Trimmed Our Tree," "Losing Everyone She Loved," "On the Wall Forever," "The Thirst for Creativity," "American Tragedy," "Harmony on the Hudson 1927," "Home After Forty-Five Years"

Muddy River Review: "I Come from Immigrants," "Time Travel"

Poetry for Ukraine: THE POET (England): "If Only My Mother Were Still Alive"

Red Eft Review: "Looking for a Happy Ending," "Only a Bed of Water Now"

Silver Birch Press: How to Heal the Earth: "A Grandmother Trying to Help the Planet"

Silver Birch Press: One Good Memory: "Dressed Alike"

Silver Birch Press: Poetry and Places: "Apple Tea in a Fairy Chimney," "Welsh Tea with Dylan Thomas," "Gondola Ride"

Verse-Virtual: "Encased in Ice," "Everything We Need," "Mourning Portrait," "Searching for My Mother's Childhood," "The Fragility of Film," "Lone Survivor"

Whispering Willow: Tree Poems: "A Grandmother Trying to Help the Planet"

Writing in a Woman's Voice: "If Only my Mother Were Still Alive," "Memory Saver"

Thanks to all my friends and family for supporting me as I wrote these poems. Special thanks to my fine art photographer son Paul Duda for designing my cover and preparing my photos, to the editors of literary journals who published many of the poems, to Andrea, Sharon, Rose Mary, and Joan, four authors who wrote wonderful blurbs, and to Karen Kelsay, editor extraordinairc, for publishing my book.

Contents

II. Loving, Losing and Lineage

*Today, it's our responsibility to further the immigrant dream.
To write, to pass on the dream and tell its truth.*
—Natalie Goldberg, *The True Sense of Writing*

Write what should not be forgotten.
—Isabel Allende

I.

Separating, Sacrificing and Surviving

The author and her parents in 1949

I Come from Immigrants

I come from Hungarians who left almost everything behind
to ensure their children had chances they only dreamt of,
as they boarded immigrant ships from Bremen to New York.

I come from a blizzard the night I was born in the city,
as my mother pushed, and my father prayed in the chapel,
because a young doctor warned him we might not survive.

I come from white leather shoes bronzed for eternity
on a base that would eventually hold my wedding photo,
but first held the portrait of a Hungarian-American family.

I come from riding my tricycle in circles as my mother
churned butter, sang Hungarian ditties, and gathered eggs
to trade for necessities in the general store during the war.

I come from a home where only Hungarian was spoken
until I was five, when English was needed for school,
and cousins were no longer the only friends I understood.

I come from Shirley Temple curls, made with strips of rags,
then unwound and brushed into ringlets on my mother's finger,
and held in place with huge bows on clips in my dark brown hair.

I come from dancing the csardas with my father, feet flying
at Hungarian weddings, or racing my father in the ocean,
my mother watching from shore, ready to call a lifeguard.

I come from picnics where men twirled slabs of bacon on sticks
over fires, dripping grease onto thick bread covered with pieces of
tomatoes, onions, and green peppers topped with chunks of bacon.

I come from a house with white siding, filled with the fragrant
      odors
of my mother's cooking, hiding me stomping barefoot on Furmint
      grapes
which my father turned into Tokaji wine, as his family did in
      Hungary.

I come from numerous moves to improve our circumstances,
but angels always followed us and trimmed our tree on Xmas eve
with ornaments and sweets, then lit the candles on the branches.

I come from immigrant parents who found the courage to leave
      Hungary
and generations of ancestors all the way back to the African
      exodus,
all of whom travel with me still as I dance the csardas, feet flying
      with joy.

Foster parents

Fostering to Freedom 1906

For the first four months
of her life, my mother,
the product of a love affair
between a Budapest governess
and a Czech policeman who
never told her he was married,
languished in an orphanage
until one day . . .

Rozsa, dark hair pulled back into a bun,
dressed like a simple country woman,
set out on her yearly pilgrimage
to the large Catholic orphanage
after visiting her sister in Budapest.
She slipped into a gray-walled
room filled with white metal cribs
and numerous sleeping children,
each protected by a wooden cross
hanging above their bed.

Rozsa and Laszlo had already taken
in two boys and a girl, all between
two and five. They were theirs now,
children she could not conceive,
but souls she could foster with love.

Clothed in a black habit, an old nun
entered the room, smiled at Rozsa,
then pointed to a four-month-old,
their newest arrival. Rozsa insisted
Laszlo said they could take no more.
The nun informed her the baby,
my mother, could only be fostered
because my grandmother bore her
out of wedlock, then escaped

19

to America, promising to send
for the child as soon as she could.

Rozsa approached the iron crib
with metal bars like a prison,
as my mother gazed up at her,
then raised her tiny arms as if
begging to be released and held.
Leaning over the bed, Rozsa drew
her close. Nestled in her arms,
the infant smiled and sighed.
Rozsa recognized a gift from God
and hoped Laszlo would understand.

As the aging, decrepit train
rattled and chugged its way
across the Great Hungarian Plain,
Rozsa rubbed the infant's back
and softly hummed a lullaby.

*In the village, the child became known
for her intelligence and loving ways.
Rozsa prayed her real mother would
forget her promise, but seventeen
years later, a ticket arrived to ship
Mama, now called Margit, to America.*

*Margit constantly cried, unwilling
to leave the only mother she knew.
Her heart breaking, Rozsa reinforced
her fledgling's natural instinct
to fly off and fulfill her potential,
convincing her that great prospects
awaited her, as ever generous Rozsa
shared her gift with future generations.*

*The author's mother at age 17 (above)
and her maternal grandmother (below)*

Coming to America

On the Bremen pier bustling with noisy immigrants,
my mother finds the ticket office and stands in a line
for Hungarians, ticket in one hand, heavy satchel
in the other, warm shawl around her thin shoulders.

Margit views her new reflection in the large window,
straight dark hair she cut to just below her earlobes,
trying to look American for her waiting mother.
Gone the waist-length braid that took years to grow.

The shipping clerk shouts, "Next!" and she moves
to the counter, offering the pre-paid ticket sent
by her mother. He asks for her sponsor, but none
was mentioned in the letter sent with the ticket.

"Anyone under eighteen needs a sponsor."
She explains she will turn eighteen in a week.
"You cannot take this ship. Rules are rules."
Margit's shoulders shake with her heavy sobs.

The old woman behind her with long white hair
braided around her head offers to sponsor her.
They both have second-class tickets and can share
a cabin. The disgruntled clerk stamps both tickets.

On board the huge iron-hulled steamship,
they find their room. Margit takes the upper
bunk, giving Mrs. Olah the bottom, marveling
at the sink with running water in their cabin.

The rumbling engines groan, the horns bellow.
The ship leaves the dock and the prow slices
through the Atlantic, heading toward the setting sun.
Margit leads her sponsor outside for a final glance.

She hears a violin playing a Hungarian folk tune,
sees dancing in steerage. "We should be there too."
Mrs. Olah chuckles. Within two days, Margit can keep
nothing down as winds hurl the ship through tall swells.

After five days, the winds calm and Mrs. Olah wishes
her a happy birthday, offering her a small, wrapped box.
Inside, Margit finds a locket on a gold-plated chain.
"For a photo of your mother who is waiting for you."

In the dining room that evening, Margit wears her gift
as waiters singing "Happy Birthday" approach her
with a cake and eighteen lit candles. Others join in.
She blows out her candles as a messenger calls her name.

She raises her hand and he places a telegram in it.
"Your mother must have remembered." Margit asks
Mrs. Olah to read the English message. She reads it
silently, then leads Margit outside to two deck chairs.

She takes her hand. "Your mother died last night, child.
She was very ill." Margit screams. First, she was left
in an orphanage and now abandoned in a strange country.
"I will be alone again." "No, your stepfather will meet you."

"I must return to Hungary." Mrs. Olah shakes her head
"Impossible. The ticket costs too much." "But I must.
Rozsa *neni* was the only mother I knew who loved me.
I never heard my mother's voice or even saw her smile."

"If you want to hear her speak, listen to your own voice.
If you want to see her smile, look in the mirror. A woman
carried you in her womb for nine months. You were one.
Now you must carry her in your heart and make her proud."

Margit watches dense sea fog slither over the ship's railing
and silently glide toward them. Hearing the baritone blast
of the foghorn, she wipes away her tears and leads her sponsor
back inside, knowing she must find the courage to survive.

The author's mother and father in 1927

Harmony on the Hudson 1927

A passenger on the first bus from Sacred Heart
Hungarian Church, my father is already on board,
balancing in the prow. His eyes, almost as dark
as his black hair, watch women hurrying toward
the Skyline at Sunset cruise from the second bus.

A slim woman with dark wavy hair in a flapper dress
with a drop waist, pleated skirt, and t-strap heels
sees him staring at her and smiles back. He moves
to help her from the pier and leads her to a seat,
taking the one beside her.

"I'm Andras," he offers in Hungarian. "Margit,
from Battonya in Bekes County," she replies.
He looks puzzled. "It's on the Great Plain. You?"
"Turterebes on the river Tur. It was given
to Romania after the war. Now it's Turulung."

Filled with passengers, the ship jolts into reverse
and pitches into the East River. Margit gulps, grabs
her seat, admits she can't swim. "I grew up swimming.
I can save you," Andras offers, smiling. A band
plays "Bye, Bye, Blackbird" as they approach
the Brooklyn Bridge and hear over the intercom:

When Roebling, the engineer, became bedridden,
his wife Emily took his place and finished the job.

"Only in America could a woman do that. My daughters
will have so many opportunities." Andras smiles again.
She was going to be a great mother. As the ship passes
New York Harbor, Margit beams at the electric lights
erupting in every high rise. "They would never believe
this in my village. It's beautiful. Wish I owned a camera."

"I like your dress," he ventures, not easily distracted.
"I'm a governess. My mistress gives me the clothes
she no longer wears and lets me attend English classes."
Beautiful and smart, he thinks. "Want to dance?"
Following him inside, she slips into his arms as the band
plays "My Blue Heaven," and she follows him easily.
"Oh, we're under the Manhattan Bridge," she exclaims,
glancing through a window. "I take a subway across that
every day to a factory where I work as an autobody man,"
he tells her, proud he has a trade. She looks impressed.

The band starts to play a csardas, a courting dance.
"Do you know it?" She smiles and nods as he
grasps her waist and her hands encircle his neck.
Others gather to watch them work through the slow *lassu*
into the exhilarating *friss* as he swings her to the finish
amid claps and cheers. Panting, he leads her to a table
by a window as a waiter brings two glasses of wine
and a plate of hot hors d'oeuvres. They approach
the Hudson River and glimpse the Statue of Liberty
shining green in the spotlights as the intercom instructs:

Notice Lady Liberty and her torch with a flame of gold.
Bertholdi used his mother's features to shape her face.

"I cried when I saw her from the deck of the ship
three years ago," Margit tells him. "My mother sent
for me, but she died before I arrived."

A man taps Andras on the shoulder. "Time."
"I'll be back," he promises, patting her hand.
He climbs to the stage. As the band breaks into
Hungarian tunes, he sings the lyrics and Margit
gasps in surprise. When the set is finished, he
rejoins her. "My foster father sang in our summer
Playhouse, but you sing, you dance, and even swim."

Andras suddenly finds the courage to tell her a secret
few others know. "I was married before. She
was to join me in America, but she died in childbirth.
I have a son back home being raised by her parents."
His words gush out. Tears stream down Margit's cheek.
"I learned what it means not to know a mother. I'm sorry."

That night, back in his room, Andras writes to his mother
to tell her he feels he has found someone to love again.

The author as an infant in her mother's arms

Flocks of Birds and Fairy Tales

They soared, a flock of birds,
dark wings blackening the sky,
squawking "Tora, Tora, Tora,"
unafraid of sleeping giants.

Just as black hawks swoop
toward prey from great heights,
torpedoes rained from planes,
bombarding every ship in port.

Bits and pieces of vessels,
like shards of broken pottery,
flew through billowing smoke
as alarms sounded too late

and twenty-four hundred sailors
were trapped or blown overboard,
suffocated below deck or
in water colored with flames.

Those of us born that year
rocked in the safety of arms,
but the *Oklahoma* capsized,
its death saving the *Maryland.*

We listened to the bluebirds sing
as anxious mothers read us fairy tales,
while the *Arizona* and the *Utah*
sank in the harbor, taking us to war.

The author's mother at age 18

A Mother's Courage

What gave you the courage
to leave a foster mother who loved you
and cross an ocean on a grand ship
to come to a mother you never met?

What gave you the courage
to leave a cruel stepfather
and become a governess
before you even spoke English?

What gave you the courage
to marry a man you met on a
Hungarian dinner-dance cruise
and start a new life together?

What gave you the courage
to get pregnant and give birth
to me, after you lost one baby
and feared losing another?

What gave you the courage,
with only six years of schooling,
to take me to a library every week
and teach me to love books as you did?

What gave you the courage
to listen when my third-grade teacher
told you I had to go to a place called college
to make sure you saved for my tuition?

What gave you the courage
to clean houses after Papa's heart attack,
then decide you could do better and open
a small Hungarian restaurant?

What gave you the courage,
after reading my first short story,
to buy me a used manual typewriter
and tell me to follow my heart?

What gave you the courage
to see that writing made me happy,
was the reason I was put on earth,
and give me the chances you never had?

The author as a baby

Lone Survivor

The one before me
was an ectopic pregnancy
surgically removed,
as they told Mama
she'd probably never
conceive again,
and Papa cried.

Eleven years later,
in a winter blizzard,
I came into the world
in a difficult birth
after they told Papa
neither Mama nor I
would survive.

Two years later,
Mama miscarried
a male infant
at five months,
her final attempt.
Whatever I did in life,
I always did for three.

The author at age 3

Amber Alert in Oswego County

Oswego evolved from the Iroquois word
OSHWEGA, meaning "pouring out place,"
referring to the mouth of the Oswego River,
which flows into huge Lake Ontario.

Oswego County was mainly farm country
where couples raised cows, crops, and children
who helped them fight one hundred fourteen
inches of dreaded snow and ice every winter.

In the midst of World War II, the large
farming families planted Victory Gardens,
recruited extra boys to help work the farms,
and gathered to picnic on the Fourth of July.

In 1944, my uncle, aunt, and six children
arrived with food and equipment for baseball,
as Papa cooked outside, Mama inside, sure
my cousins would watch me as she directed.

Finally, she called everyone to get their food,
but found I was not with my older cousins.
They said folks miles away in Black River
could hear her shrieks of agony and loss.

The box phones on wallpapered kitchen walls
rang incessantly throughout Oswego County
as news spread of the missing three-year-old
at the Hungarian's farm. Police were called.

Celebrations stopped. Carloads of volunteers
filled our yard and lined both sides of Route 2.
Neighbors we didn't know swarmed the fields
calling "Mancika," "Mancika," over and over.

They searched both fields and wooded areas.
Time passed. Light dimmed. People panicked.
Someone mentioned our stream, a tributary
of the Oswego River. Mama screamed again.

The volunteers, some with hunting dogs,
pushed toward the stream behind the barn.
They slid down a steep embankment to the bed,
flanked by muddy banks and willow trees.

They never knew who saw me first,
Tippy by my side, sitting on the bank
making mud pies in an old cupcake tin,
imitating Mama. Alerted, Tippy barked.

Mama ran toward me and gathered me up,
hugging and kissing me as my muddy hands
encircled her neck. Papa joined us as tears of joy
poured out of their eyes and down their cheeks.

My parents insisted on everyone staying
to dance, eat, and drink wine that Papa made.
A few drove home to bring contributions
to the feast and their instruments to play.

In time, harsh winters drove us from Oswego County,
but my cousin says they still talk about the child
who spoke no English and never understood
why just seeing her made everyone so happy.

The author in her go-to-meeting outfit *(above)*
and with her doll Gloria (below)

Dressed Alike

In 1946, Mama and I rode the train
to Bridgeport on alternate weekends
to see Papa, who had taken a new job.
We would join him after I finished
kindergarten. Gloria, my favorite doll,
to whom I still spoke Hungarian,
joined me on every trip to the city.

Gloria resembled me with dark hair,
softly curled on a wig of mohair,
and realistic dark glass eyes that blinked.
She had a composition head and limbs
made of sawdust, glue and cornstarch
attached to a soft, stuffed cloth torso.

Mama decided we would surprise
Papa for his birthday and sewed
matching dresses of dark gold satin
for Gloria and me on her treadle machine.
Each dress had a wide gathered collar
and puffy short sleeves and we wore
matching patent leather shoes. Mama
called them our *go-to-meeting outfits.*

Excitement started as soon as we took
our padded seats on the train
and others passed us in the aisle.
Women stopped to stare at us
and all took time to comment.

Oh, look, she is dressed like her doll.
I love the matching dresses.
You are a very lucky little girl
to have such a clever Mama.
You and your doll are so pretty.

Matching. Lucky. Clever.
I soaked up the new words,
asking Mama the meaning of each,
as I slowly learned more English
every weekend on the hissing train,
bucking us forward on rapid stops.

When we arrived, Papa was waiting
on the platform. The door was opened
and Gloria and I ran into his arms.
"You both look so pretty," Papa said.
"I have a clever Mama," I told him,
showing off new linguistic skills.
"Yes, you do, Mancika," Papa agreed,
smiling at Mama with appreciation.

Seventy-five years later, I found Gloria
tucked away safely, long curls straight
from all the brushing, minute cracks
and flaking covering face and limbs.
She still wears her go-to-meeting dress
and reminds me of all the words I learned
in English going to see Papa in Bridgeport.

Our spun glass tree topper with angel

Hungarian Angels Trimmed Our Tree

Deep inside my dream, a bell tinkles
and I hear Mama say: *"Boldog Karacsonyt,"*
wishing me a Merry Christmas. "Wake up,
little one. The angels trimmed our tree
and the baby Jesus brought you presents."

I smell candles burning, coffee brewing,
stuffed cabbage simmering.

I grab my doll Gloria, and Mama carries me
to the living room,where Papa waits
with nut and poppy seed *beigli* to eat
as Christmas carols stream from a Victrola.
The nut rolls keep trouble away,
the poppy seed brings prosperity.

After I welcome baby Jesus in the crèche,
Papa helps me open the sliding glass doors
to the front room where Gloria and I
find Christmas in the forties.

A huge evergreen fills a corner and spreads
its fragrance as Shiny Brite glass ornaments
of balls, pinecones, trees, angels and wreaths
reflect flickering candlelight on branches
draped with silver garlands and hung with
candy canes, ribbon candy, and *szaloncukor,*
Hungarian candy flavored with fondant
wrapped in colored foil. They vie for space
with walnuts Mama and I painted gold or silver.
Papa pierced the top of each with a toothpick,
to which Mama attached a ribbon for hanging.

At the peak, I find the tree topper. A circle
of spun glass and white angel hair holds
a gorgeous cardboard angel with golden wings.

I sit down on the carpet and just stare at her
high in her cloud, and let Gloria enjoy
the beauty that only angels could create.
The wrapped presents baby Jesus brought fill
the space beneath the tree and I feel like
I've gone to heaven, but that was long ago,
before I realized Mama and Papa were angels.

The author's brother as a Romanian soldier

The Fragility of Film

I always knew I had a brother named Jozsef,
although Papa told me I could call him Joey.
He was from the first reel of Papa's life
captured in eight millimeters of silence.

To avoid being drafted by the Romanians
who were awarded his part of Hungary,
Papa joined his older brother in America,
to be followed by Kati after Joey was born.

But Kati died in a long and difficult childbirth,
leaving Joey to be raised by her parents in
a section of Hungary, now Romania, which
tried to slice Magyar culture from the film.

Mama and I were from the second reel,
set in America through the Depression,
World War II, and the Iron Curtain era,
long after talkies and theaters were invented.

Joey's mustached, uniformed image framed
on my nightstand kept him in my thoughts.
I talked to Joey, prayed for Joey, and loved him
with all my heart, as only a seven-year-old can.

Unlike Papa, Joey was drafted in World War II
by Romanians who mistreated Magyar conscripts.
Papa decided to help Joey escape to America
but had to secretly send him money for bribes.

Used garments made it through inspections,
so like the director of a movie, Mama bought
tattered items of clothing at the Goodwill store
and sewed money into an old overcoat lining.

Papa sent the package to his sister, also caught
in the blurry existence of Magyars in Romania.
She tore open the lining, gingerly removing bills
as Mama had instructed. All we could do was pray.

We repeated the same prayers over and over
as if memorizing an actor's dialogue while
Papa anxiously awaited Joey's appearance,
as one awaits the opening scene of a movie.

A letter finally arrived from Papa's sister,
telling us Joey was captured at the border
and incarcerated for five years in a prison
in Russia or Romania. No one knew where.

Papa was inconsolable, crying every night.
Our life was never the same. After his release,
Joey married, had a son, and sent letters,
but never tried to escape to America again.

Joey died at fifty, leaving a wife and teenaged son
who spoke only Romanian we did not understand.
It was as if the film of Joey's existence had faded,
along with his last name, leaving only faint images
of a brother I never met but continued to love.

The Lone Ranger

He was my best friend in our small town.

Two years older than my eight years, his
stringy red hair, thick dark-rimmed glasses,
and heavy stutter made him a target for bullies,
forcing him to play with the girl next door.
I always insisted on being the Lone Ranger
and he had to settle for my sidekick Tonto
who called me Kemo Sabe, "faithful friend."
He let me wear the black mask and cowboy hat,
shoot rustlers with the silver bullets
in our pretend guns, and shout, "Hi Yo, Silver"
as we galloped away after every adventure.

Without warning, his father was transferred,
his family moved away, and he galloped
out of my life.

Years later, after a lecture in New York City,
I heard "Hi Yo, Silver" from the crowd
amidst the squawking horns of cabs and
Tower of Babel dialects. I turned and barely
recognized Tonto wearing contacts and
a tailored suit befitting the manager of a
major Savings and Loan. He couldn't believe
it was really me and invited me to lunch,
where I discovered he had overcome his stutter
as he showed me photos of his model-thin wife,
two perfect children, a house in the Hamptons.
Finally, he told me he thought of me often,
insisting I made his childhood bearable.

I should have let him be the Lone Ranger.

The author as a toddler with her dog

Memory Saver

My mother saved everything historical,
especially memories stored in photographs.
Other immigrants brought bulging satchels
filled with clothing and religious mementos.
Mama brought rare photos of her childhood.

I can see Mama as a toddler, a third grader,
dressed for her First Communion. Others
depict her foster family—parents, older sister,
and a theater group where her father acted.
She would point to each and tell me stories.

As a poor immigrant from a small village
in Hungary, Mama did not own a camera until
I was on the way, and she got a Kodak Brownie.
Others cried over World War II, but Mama said
we need photos to remember and saved moments.

I see Papa clutching me like a fragile infant,
wheeling me in a carriage with kewpie dolls,
helping me to stand, walk, ride a tricycle. You
can see me feeding chickens, playing with dogs,
holding a ball. A Kodamatic joined the Brownie.

Even in black and white, my blond hair turns dark.
I am seen wearing Shirley Temple curls, pigtails,
short, permed hair, all styles adorned with ribbons.
The child in those photos would be another stranger
lost to oblivion if Mama had not saved her on film.

I am shown biking, canoeing, hanging from swing
sets, learning to swim, listening to 45 RPM records.
There I am in a Girl Scout uniform, a skating outfit,
a prom gown my date admires. Mama missed little.
Others may scowl or squint, but I am typically smiling.

On my fifteenth birthday, Mama hands me a fancy
package to unwrap. I find a new camera and hear
we need photos to remember. The torch is passed.

The author as a teenager dancing at a nearby venue

Letter to a Faraway Friend

I finally made it, Betty.
I turned sixteen at last.
A daughter of immigrants,
I finally get to go on dates,
as I am now a woman.

After the birthday dance,
Papa gave me a used car
with a roof that folded,
and his complete trust,
as I am now a woman.

With the top down, I cruise
two Kirby and Holloways,
for shakes brought on skates
while new friends jump in,
as I am now a woman.

I drive to every dance
in a fire hall in one town,
a roller rink in another,
a church hall in a third,
as I am now a woman.

I jitterbug, do the twist,
and slow dance with dips,
as boys learn my name
and ask me for dates,
as I am now a woman.

A kiss is not enough
for those boys I reject,
remembering Papa's trust
and new obligations,
as I am now a woman.

A trombonist the author photographed
on the Mississippi river levee in New Orleans

The Hand in the River

It was the gentle sweep of his hand
as he dipped it into the Mississippi,
while I photographed the trombonist
belting out "Old Man River" on the levee.

"Is it warm or cold?" I called down.
"Warm," he replied with an accent.
I changed lenses. "Where you from?"
"Prague," he replied. Shot six more frames.

"Gorgeous city." I tipped the trombonist,
put away my gear. Saw him bound up the levee.
"You know Prague?" Disbelief in his voice.
I laughed. "I'm a travel photographer."

"Can we talk? I am Jiri." Kind eyes. "Kate."
An engineer from Communist Prague,
he lectured at a symposium in Canada,
but could only bring four hundred dollars.

After his meeting, a ten-day bus pass took him
around America for two-hundred-fifty.
He slept in the coach burning rubber by night,
and spent ten dollars a day on fast food.

I admired his ingenuity, his self-sacrifice.
He had seen more of the States than I had.
"Join me while I shoot the old cemetery
and I'll buy you dinner." A look of jubilation.

As I shot the stacked vaults of the Creoles,
and sun-bleached crypts of plantation gentry,
the syncopated rhythm of ragtime and blues
enveloped us in the City of the Dead.

Back in the Vieux Carre, I chose a lacy,
wrought-iron balcony for people-watching,
and ordered hurricanes to sip as we talked
over gumbo ya-ya and crispy fried oysters.

Jiri closed his eyes to the smooth, soulful jazz
as he savored blackened redfish smothered
in crawfish etouffee, followed by bananas foster.
Suddenly, a moan as he glanced at his watch.

"Wait, there's a shortcut." I left money on the bill,
led our way through back alleys. He retrieved his case,
handed me his number on a napkin. "Call me, Kate."
He boarded the bus, departed in a hiss of compressed air.

Too early to retire to my slave quarters B and B,
I strolled along the levee, heard the trombonist
charming even the river with his improvisations.
I smiled and planned my next assignment to Prague.

The author's paternal grandmother sitting with her rosary

Losing Everyone She Loved

She stared out the door at Janos waiting
in the cart to take her youngest son
to the train to join her oldest in America.
Wrinkles, like deep gullies, lined her face
with age, though she was barely fifty.

Grasping her rosary, she drew a shawl
over her black dress and babushka.
Istvan's death in a mill fire in America
six years ago dressed her in the black
she'd wear the rest of her life as a widow.

She was slowly losing them all. Eva and Anna,
three and one, died coughing in misery
in the influenza pandemic of '89 when
strong herbs could no longer lower fevers,
open throats. They passed, having barely lived.

She screamed over and over, pounding her heart
as they lowered a single casket holding both girls.
She cried until she was pregnant again with Gyuri,
their first son, who eventually joined Istvan on his
final trip to the dragon belching flames from its stacks.

Istvan made five one-year trips to America
leaving her happily pregnant on four.
Mari and Janos followed Gyuri, the first.
Then came Erzsi followed by Andras, the last,
resembling Istvan, morphing into her favorite.

Now he, too, prepared to leave her to avoid
the Romanian draft of young Hungarian men.
His wife would follow soon after giving birth.
He could give his life for Hungary, but never
for Romania, given their region as spoils of war.

Andras approached her carrying a satchel stuffed
with clothes, his passport, and the steerage ticket
costing thirty dollars, bought and sent by Gyuri.
She slipped a black wooden cross with a brass Jesus
off the wall and shoved it into his bulging satchel.

Promising to return as soon as he could, Andras
wrapped his long arms around her short stature.
She held him for a final time. The flu stole her babies.
Then Gyuri joined Istvan and stayed after he died.
Mari rejoined her husband in Canada. Now Andras.

"I'll never see my lambs again," she insisted,
reading the future like a Roma fortune teller.
Andras wiped his eyes. "Erzsi will care for you,
Janos will tend the land. Gyuri and I will write
and send photos and money until we return."

She only shook her head as if she had read
Gypsy tarot cards and saw the Depression,
the ravages of World War II, the Iron Curtain,
and even her own death. She had to find the
strength she had used to raise her children alone.

"Andras!" Janos shouted from the cart,
"You will miss the train to your ship."
She tried not to let him go, but go he must.
He left my grandmother memorizing his image
as she said her rosary, soliciting his safekeeping.

The author's father leading her down the aisle on her wedding day

My Father's Tears

Some men would rather die
than let others see them cry.
Others will shed tears of joy
at the slightest provocation.
My father was one of the latter.

Mama said Papa cried the first time
he saw me in her arms, as a doctor
had warned him we both might die.
After hours of prayer, he shed tears,
sure his appeals had induced a miracle.

He cried at my accomplishments—
straight A's, spelling bee winner,
sale of a short story to a journal,
full ride to the State University.
Many events triggered his tears.

On my wedding day, he entered the
Bridal Room, saw me in my gown,
and a river flowed. "I'm so proud to
be your Papa." Wiping away tears,
he smiled and led me down the aisle.

Two years later, my husband and I
carried infant twin boys off a flight
to my father, waiting at the gate.
His tears streamed. "First time he's
seen them, right?" passengers asked.

Years later, traveling through Hungary,
I heard a violin and entered a café. The
violinist grinned, pointed at me, and
played a song every Hungarian father
sings to his daughter. My tears flowed.

The author's paternal grandmother in her coffin,
with her aunt, uncle, and a few cousins behind

Mourning Portrait

Looking like Bergman's characters,
They grieve for the body in the coffin.

In the forties, it was a tradition
among Hungarian villagers
to take a mourning portrait
with relatives and close friends
gathered behind the open casket.

I have one of Papa's mother,
my grandmother Katalin,
and relatives I never met,
trapped in Transylvania, given
to Romania after World War l.

Letters, not kisses or warm hugs
were how we had exchanged longings
for one another. Mine in English,
hers in Hungarian, my parents
as translators for our words of love.

When grandmother was seventy-six,
a sepia-toned mourning portrait arrived.
A black babushka covered her hair
amidst the mountain of white lace
draped over her and the coffin.

My father's sister Erzsi dressed all in black,
and brother Janos, who most resembled Papa,
sat in the front row, the only two left at home.
Janos wore a suit that looked vaguely familiar
and was the only male wearing a regular tie.

I remembered all the boxes of
used clothing hiding paper money
Mama sewed into the thick linings
because they easily got through
the stringent customs of Romania.

Unacquainted with most of Papa's clan,
I scoured all the dejected faces for any
resemblance to me. I found none in
the expressions drooping with grief.
Papa said I looked like his mother.

Many, many years later, Papa died
suddenly of a massive heart attack.
I wrote to tell relatives in Transylvania,
the ones who might still be alive
and now spoke only Romanian.

They hired an interpreter to write to me
and ask why I sent no mourning portrait.
I wrote back, finding it hard to explain
that we take no such photos in America,
preferring to remember the dead as they lived.

I never heard from my relatives again, making
me feel as if I had robbed them of their due.
Seventy years later, I stare at the aging photo
of my grandmother and grieving kith and kin,
and lament the loss of my Hungarian family.

The author's mother and foster sister
at their First Communion (above),
and the two of them 45 years later (below)

Home After Forty-Five Years

"It's my first time back in forty-five years,"
Margit announces, wishing she could use
the loudspeaker to tell the whole airport.
"Have a wonderful trip to Hungary, my dear,"
the ticket taker says, patting the wrinkled hand
of the white-haired lady beaming with joy.

The ship had taken nine days in 1924,
the plane takes eight hours to Budapest in 69,
then the four-hour train trip to Battonya
where Mariska and two good friends wait
at the station with open arms and bouquets
of sunflowers. Margit feels like she's dreaming.

The three smother her in hugs and kisses
and versions of welcome back in Hungarian
as the conductor lowers two heavy suitcases
and smiles at their reunion. "Your hair is white,"
Mariska, her foster sister, says. "So is yours,"
Margit counters, "But I'd know you anywhere."

Margit marvels at Gerda and Agi, so unchanged
except for gray hair, but Mari has grown heavy.
"Let's go to my house," Mari says. "I have lunch
waiting." Margit hires a taxi for them and Mari
gives the driver their old address on Garmezy Street.
"I live there now. I helped Rozsa *neni* as she aged."

On either side of her, Agi and Gerda hug Margit
and marvel at how good she looks. They wear
cotton dresses longer than Margit's and smile
at her as if she is an apparition from their past.
The white stucco house with a straw roof looks
the same. It is as if Margit never left at seventeen.

They take places at the table set with hand-painted plates on an embroidered tablecloth. Mari brings a cucumber salad, then heats something on the stove. "You didn't!" "Of course I remembered your favorite and made *lecso* just like Rozsa *neni* did, but added sausage to the onions, hot peppers, and tomatoes. Have some bread and butter."

Margit finds out that all got married and had children, Mari the most with three boys and a girl. "I have one daughter, but she has three boys and a girl under four," Margit says, showing photos. "To our reunion," Margit says, raising her glass of plum brandy. When Mari brings crepes filled with fruit, Margit passes out her presents.

After lunch, Mari finds someone to photograph them under the acacia tree. "I used to resent Margit," Mari admits. "I was special, the only girl until she arrived, and then she was always smarter and prettier." Margit gasps in surprise. "She even had a mother in America who was going to send for her, but when she left, I missed her so much."

When the others leave, Margit hugs Mariska and tells her: "I never stopped loving you." "I was stupid to be jealous." "I want to see their grave," Margit says. "Tomorrow," Mari promises, "but you won't be happy. Their coffins are buried beneath six others. They claim we have no more room." "I'll fix that, but will have nightmares."

Mari insisted she stay with her as she was also widowed. In bed, they spooned as they had as children. "Zoltan and Bela?" Margit asks. "Both dead. One heart attack, one cancer. Good brothers." "Eva? Donka?" "Jewish and Roma. Gone in the camps with their whole families." Margit asks no more as tears flow down her cheeks.

In the morning, Mari walks Margit to the small cemetery
and they find flowers at the grave. "I try to bring them
flowers from the garden every week." Margit hugs her,
then joins Mari in the prayers for the dead. After paying
the caretaker, arrangements are made to construct a walled-in
gravesite Rozsa and Laszlo will never be forced to share.

The rest of the two weeks are spent visiting with friends
and Mari's children, who work as local tradesmen. They
ask Margit where she would like to go and she asks to visit
the nearby museum for Janos Arany, the Hungarian poet.
She wishes her daughter, also a writer, had been able to come,
but Margit knows she is there with her, tucked into her heart.

The following day, Mari passes her a gift to open on the train
back to Budapest. They hug farewell for what they both know
will be the last time and Margit tells her, "I never really left,
you know." "I know." In the package, Margit finds a copy of
Arany's poems and Margit comes upon the quote she memorized
in school: "In dreams and in love, there are no impossibilities."

The author's mother cooking goulash

If Only My Mother Were Still Alive

I was not surprised to see that so many Hungarians
were taking in Ukrainian refugees and making sure
they had a safe, warm place to stay and plenty to eat.

As a teen, I never knew how many were coming for dinner,
but I could be sure that no one left hungry or unhappy.
"First we eat, then we talk," my Hungarian mother would say.

My mother had always loved to cook and garden, and we had
a basement crammed with her canning jars filled with food
grown in the garden she tended with love behind our house.

When she was ready to open her little Hungarian diner,
she chose a spot across from the local air base because
seventeen thousand airmen were hungry and lonely.

She became their surrogate mother and confidante
and the diner always bulged with airmen eating goulash
and telling her their problems as she made time to listen.

If she were still alive, she'd probably get on the first plane
to Ukraine to help the civilians hiding in basements
leave the country in safety, sending most to Hungary.

And then she would ask Zelensky and Putin to dinner.
"First we eat, then we talk," she'd tell them, asking to meet
in a small restaurant that would let her cook the meal.

Chilled cherry soup with sour cream to start,
stuffed cabbage or chicken paprikash for an entrée,
and for dessert, Dobos torte with chocolate and caramel.

She always felt that anything could be solved with talk
and kindness, but not if the people were hungry, convinced
it was hard to be compassionate on an empty stomach.

"Now what is the problem, boys?" she'd ask the leaders.
"You cannot kill innocent people. Have some more
of my husband's homemade wine, eat, and tell me all."

And soon they would be discussing a cease-fire and peace.
Her food and lots of empathy were all that she would need,
If ONLY my Hungarian mother were still alive.

The author's mother as a teenager in her Confirmation dress

Searching for My Mother's Childhood

for my mother Margit 1906–1980

After her passing, many questions remain
so I go in search of my mother's childhood
on the fields of the Great Hungarian Plain.

In my lap, handcrafted wooden boxes contain
photos of family and friends left on the fertile terrain.
After her passing, many questions remain.

In her village, a thatched roof covers every stucco frame
hidden behind fences concealing each sheltered domain
on the fields of the Great Hungarian Plain.

Inside, hand-painted plates, embroidered cloths, simple games,
before sleep on the clay stove shelf listening for trains.
After her passing, many questions remain.

Her foster father, shoemaker and soloist, sang refrains
while his wife taught Mama to love and achieve her aims
on the fields of the Great Hungarian Plain.

I show the photos around, and everyone strains
but attempts to recall the girl who left are all in vain.
After her passing, many questions still remain
on the fields of Great Hungarian Plain.

American Tragedy

What if, instead of emigrating
from Hungary in the early 1920s,
my parents emigrated from Mexico
around 2005 and settled
in a Texas town called Uvalde
where I was born in 2011?
They left their lives behind
to give me chances they never had.
What if, as hoped, I excelled in school,
dreamed of becoming a teacher,
and made the honor roll every year?
What if the dreams of my parents,
along with mine, were coming true?

And then, one day, a mentally unstable
eighteen-year-old with two assault rifles,
entered the school and my classroom?
He killed two teachers, nineteen students,
and wounded numerous others.
What if I was one of the students
whose life and dreams he snubbed out
as nineteen policemen waited in the hall?

Papa, who looked most like Bogart,
but admired the tactics of Cagney,
would not have waited for two hours.
He would have found a long two-by-four,
rushed inside past the waiting policemen,
and broken through the classroom door
with inhuman strength as he was shot.
The policemen, forced into action,
finally entered and shot the killer dead.
Papa would have called my name,
scanning all the bodies of the children,

then howled in pain as he pulled my body
into his arms while his thick blood flowed,
and tears poured down his ruddy cheeks.
The EMTS would try to get him on a gurney,
but he would not release my lifeless body,
as he tried to figure out how to tell
Mama, still praying her rosary outside,
that the dream we all had was shattered.

Gifts from a Stranger

My daughter's two-year-old squirming body
felt heavy in my arms as I wove my way toward
the wooden rocker under the trees. I took the seat,
rocking her back to sleep as my cousin's wedding
music continued to play. Having the reception
outdoors was perfect for those of us with toddlers.

I searched for our five-year-old twin sons
and their younger brother and found them
in the mass of preschoolers chasing
one another among two hundred guests.
My husband waved from a group of men,
leaving me wishing I also had someone
to engage in stimulating conversation.

An older man approached me and asked if he
could take the seat next to me. "I am Geza,"
he offered. I smiled. "Margaret. Andrew was
my father." "I figured," he said. "You remind
me of Katalin, his mother." So Papa was right.
I did resemble his mother. I missed him so.

Paul, who recently turned four, ran by chasing
a small dog. "He's one of yours, isn't he?" Geza
asked. I was astonished. "How did you know?"
"He looks just like your father at that age. I come
from the same village. We were best friends."
Tears welled up in my eyes. We had much to discuss.
I had never seen any photographs of Papa as a child.

II.

Loving, Losing and Lineage

The author's graduate student husband at his desk in college

Time Travel

I've never known how
to explain how I felt
the first time I saw him
in that lecture hall.

His friend, whom I just met,
and I walked in together,
both late, neither knowing
the site had been changed.

He stood up from his seat
and started toward us with his
dark wavy hair and cleft chin.
I gasped, stifling my recognition.

Sixty years later, I still recall
feeling I knew him from
another life in another time,
a feeling I never understood.

A Slavic Rusyn, his ancestors
roamed the slopes of Carpathian
mountains and his tribe interacted
with the Magyars, my ancestors.

The two cultures socialized
and even intermarried
in the Middle Ages, mixing
their blood and DNA for all time.

I didn't know all this that night.
I only knew I would marry him
again and rejoin our lives once more
in another country centuries later.

The author's husband and father having a discussion

A Man Like No Other

It is said that to be happy as a wife,
you should marry a man like your father.

My father was a short, serious, sensitive man,
my tall husband was known for his sense of humor.

My father was hurt if I got the date of his birthday wrong.
Larry hoped everyone would forget his as he forgot theirs.

My father sang with bands and was a great dancer,
my husband, tone deaf, danced to a different drummer.

My father drove a car too fast and adored motorboats,
Larry got tickets for driving too slow and loved sailing.

My father was openly affectionate toward my mother,
my husband balked at even holding my hand in public.

My father loved jewelry and never removed his wedding ring,
Larry hated men's jewelry, refusing to wear even his wedding ring.

I am sure people wondered what attracted me to my husband, but:

Where else could I find a man whose favorite date was packing
a picnic and reading poetry to one another by a lake or stream?

Where else could I find a man who would pay fourteen dollars
a ticket in 1967 to see Joyce's *Ulysses* because I had just read it?

Where else could I find a man who loved *The Seventh Seal* by
    Bergman,
would hear a lecture on it, see the movie, and socialize over food
    to discuss it?

Where else could I find a man who admired art show openings
and would buy me an etching by Kathe Kollwitz for my birthday?

Where else could I find a man willing to stay with four
    preschoolers
and send me to a writer's conference or photo workshop for a
    week?

A friend who knew both the Rusyn and Hungarian cultures
asked me how I could be happy married to an unemotional man.

I just laughed.

Dylan's writing shed with his desk and books

Welsh Tea with Dylan Thomas

We hiked Cliff Road from Laugharne,
noticed a peregrine perched on a grassy cliff
scanning the small waders in the tidal marsh,
stalking his prey in the estuary of the Taf.

Approaching the writing shed, eggshell blue,
we peered through a small window to see where
the high school dropout composed lyrical lines
to keep southwest Wales in our minds forever.

A scarred pine table someone painted red,
three mismatched chairs, one missing slats,
crinkled strips of paper with words he loved
tacked to the simple, white-washed walls.

Windows placed to capture seascape and sunset,
light the crumpled pages of failure on the floor,
there since he and Caitlin, forever locked in conflict,
strode to Brown's Hotel for their nightly pints.

The sky turned misty, the air cold, as the
biting winds of fall pierced our jackets,
warning us to move down the footpath to
the boathouse tucked into the coastline cliff.

We approached the two-story house bought
by a patron just four years before Dylan died
of pneumonia, a morphine overdose, and
eighteen whiskies on his thirty-ninth birthday.

Pushing open the front door, we explored a museum,
the living room with his father's desk, and moved to
the dining room-tearoom that offered scones,
bara brith fruit bread, and two kinds of Welsh tea.

We opted for the small table beside a window
overlooking water birds wading in mudflats,
the only tourists to hear Dylan's voice imploring
his aging father to rage against the dying of the light.

Tea and hot scones arrived. Glancing at my husband,
I saw his eyes brimming, his mind far away,
focused on his own father trapped in dementia,
his brain turned to dust years before his body.

Sipping Glengettie tea, we watched the peregrine
as he pulled back his wings, dove toward the Taf,
and snatched a long-billed curlew for dinner.
Some deaths are easier than others.

Everything We Need

That day, we worked together
in the hay fields until lunch,
when you unharnessed Bessie
and let her graze by the wagon.

I spread out our meal on a cloth,
the bread with the sharp cheese,
the sausage, apples for dessert,
and red wine to quench our thirst.

When lunch was over, I packed up
and you removed your shoes, placing
them by the sickles. I kept mine on as
we lay down to rest before resuming.

Smiling, I thought of our family.
The children were educated,
had married well, settled down,
and nurtured children of their own.

We needed little but each other.
The bountiful harvest was good
and would add to our security
as we relaxed in the warm sun.

You kissed my forehead, then lay back
and pulled your hat down over your eyes,
using your arms to lie on like a pillow.
I cuddled beside you, my head on your chest.

We had everything we needed,
I thought, to be happy in our old age.
Enough money saved. Plenty to eat.
A lifetime of memories to ponder.

As I slowly fell into a deep sleep,
I didn't hear the cancer growing,
giving you barely six months to live,
and leaving me only poems to write.

Looking for a Happy Ending

Jack and Rose, madly in love,
are up to their necks in freezing water
after the *Titanic* hits an iceberg
and sinks on the TV screen
in our daughter's guest room.

We hold onto each other
like life rafts during six weeks
of drug trials two hours away.
On the nights I stay, you insist
we watch the *Titanic* together,
memorizing meaningful lines.

Open your eyes.
I've got everything I need
right here with me.
When the ship docks,
I am getting off with you.
Do not let go of my hand.
I will never let you go.

Did you hope that if we watched
it over and over again, the Coast Guard
would rescue Jack, too, and doctors
would find a cure for your cancer
and neither Rose nor I would
end up weeping in sorrow?

But life and movies don't always
have happy endings, as we discovered.
In the frigid water, Jack helps Rose
onto a wooden plank for one
and hangs on as long as he can,
but finally dies of hypothermia.

101

Rose is saved by a returning lifeboat,
then rescued by the steamship *Carpathia*.
You die in your own bed at home,
leaving me to sail on alone
on our own ship of dreams.

Glazed Croissants and Candlelight

People ask what I remember
about those last days. I reply:
"glazed croissants and
dancing in candlelight,"
the beginning and end of
every day filled with trauma.

Every morning I'd go and buy
a pair of warm glazed croissants
to consume with our Oolong tea.
He'd lost eighty-five pounds
in chemo, so needed the carbs
for his body, a skeleton of itself.

At the other end of the day
we sat together in the living room,
his arm around my shoulder,
listening to his favorite songs
in the soft glow of the candlelight
sending flickers of hope across walls.

If he had any energy left,
he would ask for one dance
and hold me close to his chest,
his hand wrapped around mine
as we swayed to the tempo, ending
with a kiss that might be our last.

Apple Tea in a Fairy Chimney

I feel the strength of my husband's hand,
as he leads me up the uneven steps,
carved into the side of a fairy chimney,
in the Goreme Valley of Cappadocia.

We enter a sand-colored room chiseled in tuff,
settle close on a stone ledge covered with pillows,
admire the woven carpet beneath our small table,
and inhale the aroma of traveling through time.

A sandaled Turkish waiter in a long white robe
brings apple tea in clear hourglass-shaped cups,
then lights a tall candle, smiles, and quickly ducks
back out the door beside a window with no pane.

Sixteen years after my husband's death,
I reach back across two million years. Once
again, eternity lets me feel his hand in mine
in the flickering candlelight of a fairy chimney.

The author's engagement photo with her fiancé

Gondola Ride

The narrow, pointed prow skims over reflective waterways
as the gondolier rows us past the lanterns in dark lagoons.
Your arm encircles my shoulders, your body leans into mine,
and the oarsman sings of stars in the Venetian night.
Inside towering medieval buildings rising on either side,
light escapes from slender windows, allowing us to peer inside.
White-haired couples hold hands, young adults kiss and dance,
and children laugh as they dash through the moments of life.
The paddle stops. We drift, gazing wide-eyed into the future,
realizing they are all ours, all the generations
we inaugurated on our forty-four-year wedded journey.
We beam at each other, hearts filled with wonder and gratitude
until the gondolier instructs me to debark alone at the next stop.
My grief and anguish is what I will now pay for our unfailing love
until the day the gondolier returns, and you reach out your hand.
I will say "Yes" again, step gingerly in, settle close to your body
and listen to the splash of the oar as the gondolier steers us both
        toward home.

The Thirst for Creativity

Every morning I rise and hurry to my desk,
hair pulled back with a ribbon, and barefoot,
thirsting for and craving the right words
to create something truly memorable.

Dry as dust, lusting for ingenuity,
unable to replenish my cerebral cortex,
seat of reasoning, fed by my senses,
armed with billions of neurons.

It is linguistic originality that I seek,
artistic cleverness and revitalization,
new inspiration for my imagination,
leading to higher-level innovation.

Hoping for stimulation, I reach for my cup,
tilt it toward my parched and withered lips,
and eagerly gulp down the coffee elixir
to summon new words and awaken a muse.

The First and Final Flakes

Before a blanket of white covers bare trees,
I wait for the first speck of dust or pollen
catching water molecules, then freezing fast
before falling on my cheek, welcoming winter.

Sculpted by chance in six-fold symmetry,
order out of disorder, yet each flake unique,
crystal hexagons melting my heart with joy,
bringing winter peace for rest and renewal.

Months from now, overcast, somber skies will escort
a final squall to cover the slush, animal spoors,
boot prints, and tire tracks, while a final flake
celebrates the last snow of spring and new growth.

Encased in Ice

Warnings sound
to stay at home as
a ten-hour ice storm
approaches.

The first pellets
hit the ground,
camouflaging
their entrance in the veil
of night and freezing rain.

Dark clouds conceal
the sunrise but not
the shiny layer forming
on snow, walks, driveway.

Birds and squirrels disappear.

As the long hours pass,
the icy sheen thickens,
fills with artistic designs,
and locks me in,
an elderly prisoner
in my own home.

Icicles form and hang.
A transparent layer coats
limbs of trees and bushes.

By the tenth hour
the road is crusted
in ice and snow.
A red truck pulls up
in front of my house.

My snow crew descends,
but not with shovels,
with salt.

Within an hour,
ice holding me captive
starts to bubble
and release me
as if telling me,
Covid is enough.

The Theft of Time

I am hanging by my fingertips
on the gnarled edge of time,
waiting for age, masked in black,
to steal what little life is left.

First it takes my energy, my memory,
wasting my minutes, days, weeks,
giving me no choice as it forces me
to rest while recharging my mind.

It leaves me with only regret
for words unsaid, books unread,
thoughts unsavored, trips untaken,
lines unwritten, hugs ungiven.

Another day, my last? "No," I yell,
"It's mine, not yours, not yet."
I still need time to rest, to think,
to write, to read, to bond, to love.

Parents, friends, even my husband
gone forever, unable to communicate,
but somehow urging me to finish,
not to fear as they await my arrival.

But I want to remain, to write more,
to experience more and even greet
great-grandchildren before my being
loses its grasp and has to fly away.

A Grandmother Trying to Help the Planet

With my advanced age and seven grandchildren,
I often worry about the world my generation
is leaving for our descendants and what more
we can do to help them inherit a better one.

Shorter and weaker than I used to be, I still leave
a carbon footprint destroying the planet I love.
Too arthritic to hike and too unsteady to bike,
I look for new ways to reduce, reuse, and recycle.

I limit my driving to necessary trips and events
and lower thermostats for both heat and cold air.
I am a vegan, trying to save animals I love from pain
and the environment from greenhouse gas emissions.

I refuse to use plastic containers that cannot be recycled
or to spray toxic pesticides linked to cancer on my weeds.
I continually downsize items I no longer want, need, or use,
giving them to the less fortunate or to sales for charities.

I travel less, using a train or a bus instead of a plane,
donate to organizations that clean up the oceans,
give clean water to villages in impoverished nations,
and attempts to save animals on the verge of extinction.

But frequent fires and floods still demolish thousands
of acres of forests, vineyards, entire communities
as tornados and hurricanes destroy all in their path
while ice caps melt, sea waters rise, droughts starve.

How will my grandchildren remember me as they sit
beneath the tree I bought each of them for Xmas this year?
Will they enjoy its shade, singing birds, scampering wildlife,
and remember I loved the earth I left them and tried to help?

On the Wall Forever

We are all there; four generations
grasping the iron railing of the watercraft
as my parents did on the steamships
that brought them to New York Harbor
as Hungarian immigrants in the twenties.

We gasp at the oxidized green statue
of Libertas, Roman Goddess of Freedom,
twenty-two stories high, gift from France
for our alliance in the Revolution, holding
the torch of freedom, now covered in gold,
and the Book of Law dated July 4, 1776.

Due to Covid, we cannot climb 393 steps
into the crown but still admire the face
that Bartholdi modeled after his mother.
I remember the first time my parents
brought me to see her when I was only
eight, and they explained how they cried
at the first sight of her guarding the harbor
and the freedoms they sought and found.

All seem so young this misty morning.
Mama has no gray hair, Papa no arthritic limp.
Larry and I are still thin and dark-haired
and our four children, the neurologist, fine art
photographer, businessman, and pediatrician
all look as they did in their thirties. But our
seven grandchildren—the lawyer, the dentist,
the writer, the engineer, the cognitive scientist,
the marine biologist, the medical researcher---
all look as they do today, healthy and hopeful.

The boat Larry hired for a private tour before
other tourists arrive, stops and Mama brings
out the walnut, raspberry, and *lekvar kiflis*
she made and passes them around as Papa
fills wine glasses with his latest vintage.
We toast the Lady and the couple who left
their rural villages where they were only
allowed six years of schooling, and came
to America to give their descendants
the chance for education they never had.

Larry and I bring out our own contribution,
a Hungarian band who had been hiding inside.
We tell Mama and Papa it is time to dance
the csardas. They beam and dance as Papa
spins Mama around, her feet and dress flying.
Then Papa asks me to dance and Mama asks
Larry, refusing to listen to his objections as
she patiently teaches him the simple steps.
The younger ones watch, then try it themselves,
and soon everyone is twirling to the folk tunes
and my photographer son records it all.

Forced to move on, the boat docks at Ellis Island.
The younger ones tell my parents to debark first,
letting Papa explain how he had to pass medical
exams and answer questions in the Registry Room,
now part of the National Museum of Immigration.
We promise to let them explore as soon as it opens.

We move to a certain area with a curved wall
of panels with thousands of names. Still early,

we are the only visitors at this hour. I ask
my parents to find their names on the panels
along the Immigrant Wall of Honor. They look
shocked, but with the help of their descendants,
finally find their names and country of origin.
Papa cries with joy, and Mama kisses me. Ever
the practical one, she asks my photographer son
to take a *photo to remember.* As he does every
Christmas, he finds a place to set his camera,
arranges the family, sets the self-timer, and steps
into the group as we smile and wait. I hear the click
of the camera as my alarm goes off and I wake up,
still smiling.

Ocean waves coming to shore

Only a Bed of Water Now

Undulating ocean waves
come splashing to shore,
bringing shells, stones,
multi-colored sea glass.

They both had to cross it,
my father in steerage,
my mother in second class,
to meet and make a new life.

Married, they lived near it
and I still say I heard waves
crashing as I was pushed
through the narrow canal.

Many years later, we approach
the time to spread ashes on the bed
of water my parents had to cross
so that waves can rock me to sleep.

Photo by Paul Duda

About the Author

Born a child of Hungarian immigrants, Margaret Duda grew up bi-lingual and bi-cultural. She could not speak English until she had to go to kindergarten, but then loved reading and had a poem in the *National Anthology of High School Poetry* at 15 and sold her first short story to a national magazine at 17. In her senior year, she wrote a weekly column for the local newspaper on school news.

She graduated from the University of Delaware, where she majored in English Literature and minored in Philosophy, winning both the Mary Healey Ford Award and the Penwoman's Bowl award for her short fiction. She was also chosen *Mademoiselle's* college representative from the University of Delaware for her articles. During summer vacations, Margaret worked as a journalist for the *Delaware State News* and interviewed people such as John F. Kennedy when he ran for President.

After graduation from college, marriage, and four children, she wrote short stories and articles for literary magazines such as *The Kansas Quarterly, The University Review, The Michigan Quarterly Review, The South Carolina Review, The Green River Review, Fine Arts Discovery,* and others. One of her stories made the Distinctive list of *Best American Short Stories.* Margaret also published over a hundred nonfiction articles and five books, had a play produced in Michigan, and since Covid, has had poems in the *Lothlorien Poetry Journal, The Muddy River Review, Verse-Virtual, Writing in a Woman's Voice, Silver Birch Press, Red Eft Review,* and six anthologies here and abroad.

She also took travel photos for the *New York Times* for ten years, traveling to forty countries and thirty-eight states, and is on the fifth and final draft of a novel about an immigrant family set in a steel mill town in the Mon Valley south of Pittsburgh, for which she won the Lucretia V. Simmons writing grant from the AAUW. Margaret was listed in an anthology of *Who's Who in Emerging Writers in 2021* and nominated for the Pushcart Prize in 2022.